Franz Josef
HAYDN

Georg Philipp
TELEMANN

Johann Friedrich
FASCH

THREE CONCERTI

for TRUMPET *and* ORCHESTRA

To access audio visit:
www.halleonard.com/mylibrary
Enter Code
3668-5472-9763-9682

ISBN: 978-1-59615-416-2

MMO **Music Minus One**

EXCLUSIVELY DISTRIBUTED BY

HAL•LEONARD®

7777 W. BLUEMOUND RD. P.O. BOX 13819 MILWAUKEE, WI 53213

Visit Hal Leonard Online at
www.halleonard.com

T0068443

CONTENTS

Performance notes by Brian Rood.

A NOTE ON THE SOLO PARTS

Because these concerti were originally composed for (and are commonly performed on) either the E-flat or D trumpet, we have included the original part for each concerto, as well as a version for the more common B-flat trumpet.

CONCERTO
for TRUMPET *&* ORCHESTRA
E-FLAT MAJOR ♯ Es-DUR
HobVIIe:1

TRUMPET IN E♭

Franz Josef Haydn
(1732-1809)
Composed 1796

Clear tonguing, excellent control, and beauty of sound are crucial to performing this movement with ease. Range is also a concern, as there are extended passages above the staff. My advice for students of all ages is to spend enough time on the basics so that one can approach this piece with joy and anticipation. Study this concerto by listening to the orchestral accompaniment, too, in order to better understand how the solo lines fit into Haydn's musical plan. A cadenza is appropriate at the end of this movement.

MMO 3801

II.

Andante cantabile

This movement is arguably the most requested selection of audition committees and music schools alike. Haydn gives the performer ideal opportunities to play simple yet gorgeous melodies. Strive for a rich and singing sound regardless of whether you use the B-flat or E-flat trumpet. Those who wish to perform this on the E-flat trumpet might consider practicing this movement on the B-flat trumpet to emulate the rich and full sound of that instrument. Consider playing vocalises and other songs on either trumpet to acquire a more song-like quality. Use your voice to sing beautifully, as this will assist your musical understanding and improve your tone on the trumpet at the same time!

III.

8

CADENZA

CONCERTO
for TRUMPET *&* ORCHESTRA
E-FLAT MAJOR ❧ Es-Dur
HobVIIe:1

TRUMPET IN B♭

Franz Josef Haydn
(1732-1809)
Composed 1796

Clear tonguing, excellent control, and beauty of sound are crucial to performing this movement with ease. Range is also a concern, as there are extended passages above the staff. My advice for students of all ages is to spend enough time on the basics so that one can approach this piece with joy and anticipation. Study this concerto by listening to the orchestral accompaniment, too, in order to better understand how the solo lines fit into Haydn's musical plan. A cadenza is appropriate at the end of this movement.

MMO 3801

II.

Andante cantabile

This movement is arguably the most requested selection of audition committees and music schools alike. Haydn gives the performer ideal opportunities to play simple yet gorgeous melodies. Strive for a rich and singing sound regardless of whether you use the B-flat or E-flat trumpet. Those who wish to perform this on the E-flat trumpet might consider practicing this movement on the B-flat trumpet to emulate the rich and full sound of that instrument. Consider playing vocalises and other songs on either trumpet to acquire a more song-like quality. Use your voice to sing beautifully, as this will assist your musical understanding and improve your tone on the trumpet at the same time!

III.

CONCERTO
for TRUMPET *&* ORCHESTRA
D MAJOR ❦ D-DUR

TRUMPET IN D

Georg Philipp Telemann
(1681-1767)

One measure of taps (two taps) precedes music

Many performers prefer to use the piccolo trumpet in A as opposed to larger instruments such as the D trumpet for Baroque works such as the Telemann and Fasch. Regardless of which instrument you use, aim for a light, almost flute-like quality. Play simple melodies and relatively easy pieces on the piccolo trumpet to help become acquainted with this pleasing but difficult instrument. If you are new to the piccolo trumpet spend just a few minutes a day at first with it.

(*Trumpet Tacet during Second Movement*)

Two measures of taps (two taps) precede music

III.

To help convey a light approach, tongue the sixteenth notes in a smooth and connected manner with consistent airflow. The eighth notes can be short but should be gently tongued without disrupting the airflow. In this movement, as well as the first one, study the melodic rhythm. By note-leading past beat and bar lines, the music will begin to take on an effortlessly rhythmic feel.

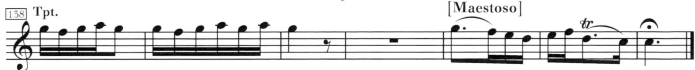

CONCERTO
for TRUMPET *&* ORCHESTRA
D MAJOR ⧓ D-DUR

TRUMPET IN B♭

Georg Philipp Telemann
(1681-1767)

One measure of taps (two taps) precedes music

Many performers prefer to use the piccolo trumpet in A as opposed to larger instruments such as the D trumpet for Baroque works such as the Telemann and Fasch. Regardless of which instrument you use, aim for a light, almost flute-like quality. Play simple melodies and relatively easy pieces on the piccolo trumpet to help become acquainted with this pleasing but difficult instrument. If you are new to the piccolo trumpet spend just a few minutes a day at first with it.

(Trumpet Tacet during Second Movement)

III.

Two measures of taps (two taps) precede music

To help convey a light approach, tongue the sixteenth notes in a smooth and connected manner with consistent airflow. The eighth notes can be short but should be gently tongued without disrupting the airflow. In this movement, as well as the first one, study the melodic rhythm. By note-leading past beat and bar lines, the music will begin to take on an effortlessly rhythmic feel.

CONCERTO
for TRUMPET *&* ORCHESTRA
D MAJOR 🎺 D-DUR

TRUMPET IN D

One measure of taps (four taps) precedes music

Johann Friedrich Fasch
(1688-1758)

This movement is fun to perform, full of challenges, and then is over before you know it! Plenty of upper-register development is needed to play this successfully. Spend time on the bigger trumpets such as the B-flat to work on fluency and consistency in the range above high C. There are plenty of good etudes available to assist you in preparing for works such as the Fasch. Aim to play this movement with two big beats to the measure, as opposed to four. This feeling of being "in two" will help the music to fly and soon you will forget how difficult this movement can be!

II.

One measure of taps (three taps) precedes music

A sweet, flute-like tonal quality is the goal here. Smooth tonguing and consistent airflow make this more enjoyable. Try playing this movement as written on the B-flat, then D, and finally the piccolo trumpet to develop more confidence and security in playing the upper notes, particularly towards the end.

III.

One measure of taps (three taps) precedes music

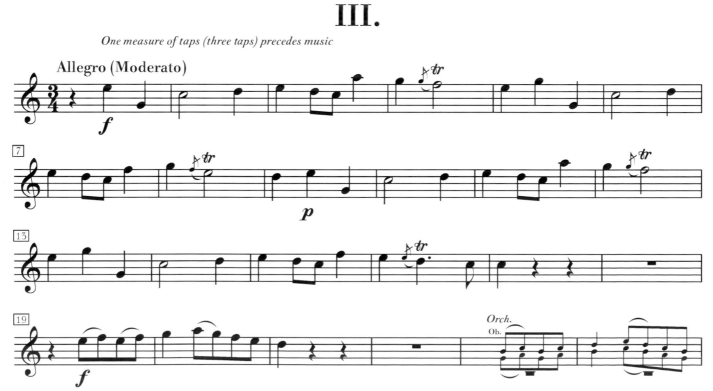

This movement has a dance-like quality and should be felt in "one." Once you have control over the rhythmic patterns try to lose the beat and bar lines in your mind. Use your creativity to explore ways to keep the music alive! The goal here is to have fun. By this I mean that you should have fun performing and your audience should enjoy listening to you. In order to accomplish this one must be as prepared as possible.

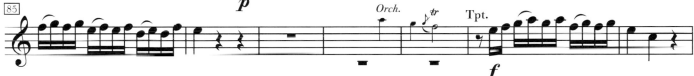

CONCERTO
for TRUMPET *&* ORCHESTRA
D MAJOR ❧ D-DUR

TRUMPET IN B♭

One measure of taps (four taps) precedes music

Johann Friedrich Fasch
(1688-1758)

This movement is fun to perform, full of challenges, and then is over before you know it! Plenty of upper-register development is needed to play this successfully. Spend time on the bigger trumpets such as the B-flat to work on fluency and consistency in the range above high C. There are plenty of good etudes available to assist you in preparing for works such as the Fasch. Aim to play this movement with two big beats to the measure, as opposed to four. This feeling of being "in two" will help the music to fly and soon you will forget how difficult this movement can be!

II.

One measure of taps (three taps) precedes music

A sweet, flute-like tonal quality is the goal here. Smooth tonguing and consistent airflow make this more enjoyable. Try playing this movement as written on the B-flat, then D, and finally the piccolo trumpet to develop more confidence and security in playing the upper notes, particularly towards the end.

III.

One measure of taps (three taps) precedes music

This movement has a dance-like quality and should be felt in "one." Once you have control over the rhythmic patterns try to lose the beat and bar lines in your mind. Use your creativity to explore ways to keep the music alive! The goal here is to have fun. By this I mean that you should have fun performing and your audience should enjoy listening to you. In order to accomplish this one must be as prepared as possible.

Engraving: Wieslaw Novak

Music Minus One is pleased to present three of the quintessential concerti for trumpet and orchestra. All of them showcase the trumpet's technical and tonal beauties in classic works from both the late Baroque and the Classical eras.

FRANZ JOSEF HAYDN (1732-1809), one of the great names in musical history, is probably the man most strongly identified with the cementing of the classical style. His studies of the groundbreaking music of Carl Philipp Emanuel Bach and his long association with Prince Esterházy allowed him to both write prolifically and expand his musical language tremendously. The result was a musical contribution to the latter eighteenth century music matched only by Mozart.

Haydn's Trumpet Concerto in E-flat major remains one of those most delightful and well-known works for the trumpet. In it, Haydn utilizes simple melodies and allows them to bring out the trumpet's most beautiful qualities. Haydn wrote this for his friend Anton Weidinger, a Viennese court trumpeter and inventor, in 1796. It was specifically written to display Weidinger's new keyed trumpet, which allowed for an uncompromised melodic line; previous trumpets were limited in their musical capabilities because of the absence of the keys which we now take for granted. Weidinger gave the premiere of the concerto in 1800.

GEORG PHILIPP TELEMANN (1681-1767) is of course one of the great names in the legion of trumpet composers. A child prodigy who was forbidden to study music, his persistence and talent nevertheless prevailed. Though he continued his study of law, his compositions continued to greater and greater acclaim, and eventually he became fast friends with Johann Sebastian Bach, and in fact became godfather to Carl Philipp Emanuel Bach.

This esteemed concerto in D major was written for trumpet, two oboes, strings and continuo. The trumpet is tacit during the middle movement of this three-movement work.

JOHANN FRIEDRICH FASCH (1688-1758) was an influential composer, though none of his music was published during his lifetime. His esteem can be measured in that other composers, such as J.S. Bach, kept manuscript copies of his works. Fasch represents an important segue between the Baroque and classical styles, and his elegant orchestrations are evident in this trumpet concerto, which, like the Telemann, is in D major and in three movements (though the trumpet again plays in all movements).

This MMO learning and performance edition includes a beautiful, authoritative, newly engraved score which gives the parts for each concerto's native-keyed (E-flat or D) trumpets as well as a version modified for the range of the commonly encountered B-flat trumpet. Listen to virtuoso Brian Rood as he plays these classic concerti, then you step center-stage to wow the crowds under the baton of Maestro Emil Kahn and the Stuttgart Festival Orchestra!